# ONE DISH VEGAN COOKBOOK

100 EASY, HEALTHY & SATISFYING MEALS FOR VEGANS IN ONE PAN, ONE BOWL OR ONE DISH

Printed in the United States of America.
First Printing, 2013

## Table of Contents

# Introduction

In our modern world, disease and major health concerns are on the rise. Obesity rates are increasing, as well as many serious health conditions such as heart disease, diabetes, cancer, and auto-immune diseases. As these diseases become more prevalent, people are looking for ways to improve their health, and the typical treatment is to turn to medication and medical treatments.

Other people are looking to figure out the root of the problem, instead of simply turning to medications for every symptom that they have. As the search continues, it has been found that there is one common theme that has a strong effect on overall health: the types of foods that a person chooses to eat.

Research studies have shown that a diet high in animal products, such as meat and dairy foods, have been linked with a higher prevalence of serious health conditions such as heart disease and cancer. People who eat less meat, or no meat at all, tend to have better health and a longer lifespan.

When people really start to understand these facts and how much their health is at risk, they may make the decision to make different food choices and cut back on meat consumption. But, there is a big difference between making the decision and actually implementing it in your life. The problem that people often run into is the fact that they are unsure about meal planning without meat or dairy, because most modern meals are centered around a meat dish.

Additionally, people often feel that planning a vegan meal takes a lot of preparation and time to fix something tasty and filling. But, the truth is that there are many delicious dishes that can be prepared without meat or any type of animal product.

I put this book together to bridge the gap, and help people find easy ways to integrate vegan eating into their daily lifestyle. These dishes are tasty, healthy and easy to make. They are designed to be "One Dish Meals," which means that they are filling enough to be served on their own-- there is no need to plan 2 or 3 side dishes with each meal. Instead, you can prepare one recipe for dinner and it will be enough to satisfy your taste buds and satisfy your hunger at the same time.

One of the biggest advantages to a One Dish Meal is the fact that it saves a lot of time and energy. Instead of working in the kitchen to prepare multiple dishes, you can save your time and prepare just one tasty meal. There are different types of meals in this book, including slow cooker meals, stove top meals, and oven baked meals.

I have found joy in cooking vegan meals for my friends and family, and I love the surprised reactions when people learn that the entire meal was prepared without animal products. These recipes are better for your health, and they are better for the environment because they don't use meat.

A few notes about common ingredients:

There are some common ingredients that you will see in the recipes, such as beans of different varieties. The convenient way to prepare beans is by use canned beans, but not all people like to use canned food. If you are making the beans from scratch, 1 can of beans equals about 1 1/2 cups. If the ingredient list does not specify the can size, then it is always the standard size of cans, and substitutions can be made based on 1 can = 1 1/2 cups. Also, anytime you are using beans, always drain the liquid from the can and rinse well before using in the recipe. The rinsing helps to decrease the juices that causes digestive bloating and gas when the beans are eaten.

Another thing to keep in mind is the fact that a few recipes call for egg replacer, vegan cheese, or other vegan products. These products can be found at any health food store, and there are many mainstream grocery stores that now offer vegan products as well. It's up to you to decide on the brand that you prefer, there are many product brands to choose from.

Many of the recipes call for vegetable broth or vegetable bouillon. Be careful about the type of bouillon that you buy, because if it is chicken or beef flavor then you can assume that it contains animal products. Read the labels to make sure it is vegan.

My wish is that you enjoy these recipes as much as I do. There are many delicious dishes that will quickly become favorites of your family!

# Slow Cooker Vegan Meals

The slow cooker is a great tool to use because of the convenience of adding everything in the pot and then forgetting about it for a few hours. It has been said that the slow cooker is the busy person's best friend, because it allows you to prepare a healthy and tasty meal without slaving over the stove all day.

Another reason I love my slow cooker is because of the fact that it gives me the opportunity to prepare hot meals in the summer without heating up the house by turning on the oven. It is great to prepare the meal ahead of time, and then come home and find that dinner is ready because it was cooking while you were gone.

These recipes offer a variety of options, including soups, stews, and many other yummy dishes. They are all vegan, and loaded with healthy ingredients such as fruits, vegetables, and whole grains.

Keep in mind that each slow cooker is unique. Some slow cookers run a little hotter than others, so if you are making the recipe for the first time it's a good idea to check on it every now and then to see how the cooking is progressing. The cooking times and temperatures are approximate and based on the average slow cooker. You may need to adjust your cooking time depending on the temperature of your slow cooker.

# Vegetable and Wild Rice Soup

## Ingredients:

1/2 cup uncooked wild rice

2 tablespoons extra virgin olive oil

6 cups vegetable broth

1/2 cup celery, chopped

1/2 cup onion, minced

1 cup zucchini, chopped

1/2 cup carrots, chopped

1/2 cup sliced almonds

Sea salt and black pepper, to taste

## Directions:

In a skillet, heat the oil and sauté the rice for 6 minutes. Scoop the rice into the slow cooker, then add the carrots, celery, onion, and broth.

Cook on low for 4 hours. Add the zucchini, then cook for 1 more hour. Season with salt and pepper according to taste. Garnish each bowl with almonds before serving.

# Cornbread and Beans

## Base Ingredients:

1 red bell pepper, chopped

1 sweet onion, chopped

3 garlic cloves, minced

1 can black beans

1 can garbanzo beans

1 can red kidney beans

1 can diced tomatoes with chilies

8-10 oz tomato sauce

1/2 can cream corn

2 teaspoons chili powder

2 teaspoons sea salt

1 teaspoon black pepper

1 teaspoon hot sauce

## Cornbread Ingredients:

1/2 cup flour

1/2 cup corn meal

1 1/4 teaspoons baking powder

1 teaspoon sea salt

1 tablespoon sugar

3/4 cups almond milk

1 egg replacer

1 1/2 tablespoons vegetable oil

1/2 can cream corn

## Directions:

Prep bell peppers and onions by chopping them, and mince the garlic. Sautee on the stove top, then add to the slow cooker.

Prep the beans by rinsing and draining them. Add beans to the slow cooker, along with the tomato sauce, tomatoes, 1/2 can of corn, hot sauce, and spices.

Put slow cooker lid in place, turn temperature to high and cook for an hour.

While the beans are cooking, mix the cornbread in a mixing bowl. Add all cornbread ingredients and stir well. After the beans have cooked for an hour, stir the slow cooker mixture. Then, spoon the cornbread mixture evenly over the top of the bean mixture.

Replace the lid, and cook for another 2 hours. It is done as soon as the cornbread is cooked through. Serve immediately.

# Slow Cooker Lentil Chili

## Ingredients:

2 onions, chopped

2 carrots, chopped

8 cloves of garlic, minced

1 stalk of celery, chopped

1 tablespoon olive oil

2 tablespoons chili powder

2 teaspoons cumin powder

1 teaspoon oregano

1 teaspoon coriander powder

1 teaspoon dry mustard

3 1/2 cups crushed tomatoes

1/2 teaspoon of seas salt (or to taste_

2 cups dry lentils

7 cups vegetable broth

## Directions:

In a large pot, add the oil, garlic, onions, celery and carrots. Sautee to soften the onions and carrots, about 4 or 5 minutes. Next, add in the spices, stir well and cook for another 2 minutes.

Prepare the lentils by rinsing them well, picking out any stones, and drain well.

Add the lentils, sautéed vegetables, tomatoes, and broth to the slow cooker.

Cook on low for 6 hours. Watch the liquid level, and add more broth if needed.

# Mexican Black Beans and Quinoa

## Ingredients:

1 orange bell pepper, chopped

3 cups water

3 garlic cloves, minced

1 1/2 cups cooked black beans

1 1/2 cups tomatoes, diced

3/4 cup quinoa, rinsed well

1 tablespoon vegetable bouillon

2 teaspoons chili powder

1/2 teaspoon cumin

Dash of salt and pepper

## Directions:

Add everything except the quinoa into the slow cooker. Cook on a low temperature for 8 hours. An hour before serving. Stir in the quinoa. It is done when you see white tails of quinoa.

# Cajun Quinoa Jambalaya

## Ingredients:

1 bell pepper, chopped

3 garlic cloves, minced

1 cup chickpeas

3 cups water

1 can diced tomatoes

1 tablespoon vegetable bouillon

2 teaspoons Cajun  seasoning

1/4 teaspoon liquid smoke

1/4 teaspoon smoked paprika

3/4 cup quinoa, well rinsed

Dash of salt and pepper

Splash of Tabasco, to taste

## Directions:

Add everything except the quinoa to the slow cooker. Cook on low for 8 hours. An hour before serving, stir in the quinoa. You will know that it is done when the quinoa separates and you can see the white tails of the quinoa.

# Rice and Pinto Beans

## Ingredients:

1 bag dried pinto beans (16 ounces)

3 garlic cloves, minced

1/3 cup picante sauce

1 tablespoon chili powder

1 teaspoon garlic powder

1/2 teaspoon cumin

1/2 teaspoon pepper

2 1/2 teaspoons sea salt

1/2 teaspoon oregano

3 bay leaves

1 cup cooked short grain brown rice

## Directions:

Rinse beans well, and pick out any rocks or wrinkled beans.

In the slow cooker, add everything except the rice. Add in enter water to cover the beans with an extra 1 - 2 inches of water over the top of the beans.

Cook on high for 4 - 5 hours, until the beans are tender. Add more water if needed.

When the beans are cooked thoroughly, add in the rice and cook for another hour to warm the rice and incorporate seasonings.

# Spicy Mango Black Beans

## Ingredients:

1 tablespoon extra virgin olive oil

2 cloves garlic, minced

1 red bell pepper, chopped

1 onion, chopped

1 teaspoon fresh ginger, finely shredded or minced

1 jalapeno, seeds removed and minced

1/2 teaspoon ground allspice

1/2 teaspoon ground cumin

1/2 teaspoon dried oregano

2 cans black beans

1 cup water

1/2 teaspoon salt

1/4 teaspoon freshly ground black pepper

1/2 teaspoon brown sugar

3 cups cooked brown rice

2 mangoes, peeled and diced

## Directions:

In a skillet, heat the oil and add the onion, garlic, bell pepper, and jalapeno. Cook for about 4 - 5 minutes until the vegetables are soft. Add in all of the seasonings, and sauté for another 2 minutes.

Add the sautéed vegetables into the slow cooker, along with the water, beans, and sugar. Stir everything together.

Place the lid on the slow cooker, and cook for 8 hours on a low temperature. Then, add in the mangoes and rice, and cook for another 30 minutes to warm.

# Spinach and Tomato Soup

## Ingredients:

1 small bag of baby spinach

1 onion, chopped

2 carrots, diced

2 celery stalks, chopped

1 clove of garlic, minced

2 cans diced tomatoes (28 ounces), juice included

4 cups vegetable broth

1 tablespoon dried basil

2 bay leaves

1/2 teaspoon crushed red pepper flakes

1 teaspoon dried oregano

## Directions:

Add everything to the slow cooker, cook on low for 10 hours. Remove bay leaves before serving.

# Tomato Ginger Chickpeas

## Ingredients:

1 tablespoon olive oil

4 cloves of garlic, minced

1 large onion, chopped

2 tablespoons ginger, minced

2 teaspoons balsamic vinegar

1 teaspoon salt

1 teaspoon ground cumin

1/2 teaspoon black pepper

2 cans chickpeas, rinsed and drained

2 cans diced tomatoes

A few large handfuls of baby spinach

2 celery ribs, chopped

chopped green onion

## Directions:

On the stovetop, over medium-high heat sauté the olive oil, onion and garlic for 5 minutes. Add in the ginger, salt, cumin, and pepper. Continue cooking for another 60 seconds.

Add everything except the green onion to the slow cooker, and cook on low for 6 hours. When serving, garnish with fresh green onions.

# Split Pea Soup

## Ingredients:

6 cups water

2 cups dry split peas

1 onion, chopped

2 stalks celery, chopped

1 carrot, chopped

1/4 teaspoon thyme

1 bay leaf

1 dash red pepper

salt and pepper

## Directions:

Rinse the split peas, and pick out rocks. Add everything in the slow cooker, cook on low for 8 hours. When the vegetables are soft, use a hand blender to blend the soup to desired consistency, then serve.

# Slow Cooker Curry

## Ingredients:

4 potatoes, peeled and diced

2 onions, chopped

2 cans tomatoes with green chilies

1 can kidney beans

1 can chickpeas

2 tablespoons olive oil

1 tablespoon curry powder

1/2 teaspoon ginger

1/2 teaspoon cardamom

2 cups cooked basmati rice

## Directions:

On the stove top, heat the oil and sauté spices and onion for 4 minutes. Add the onions to the slow cooker, along with all other ingredients. Cook on low for 8 hours. Stir in rice for the last hour to heat the rice.

# Corn and Black Bean Soup

## Ingredients:

1 tablespoon olive oil

4 cloves of garlic, minced

2 carrots, chopped

1 green bell pepper, chopped

1 onion, chopped

1 can diced tomatoes, undrained

2 cans black beans, drained and rinsed

4 cups vegetable stock

2 bay leaves

1 teaspoon dried thyme

1 teaspoon ground cumin

2 teaspoons fresh lemon juice

1/4 teaspoon cayenne pepper, more if desired

salt and ground pepper

**Directions:**

Heat the oil in a skillet, add in the carrot, onion, garlic and bell pepper. Sauté for 5 minutes.

Add the sautéed vegetables into the slow cooker, add all other ingredients except the lemon juice into the slow cooker.

Cook on low for 8 hours, or high for 4 hours. Remove the bay leaves and stir in the lemon juice before serving.

# Vegan Stew

## Ingredients:

1 quart vegetable broth

1 lb firm tofu

1 onion, chopped

5 tablespoons vegan Worcestershire sauce

2 cloves of garlic, minced

1 tablespoon soy sauce

4 potatoes, peeled and diced

4 carrots, chopped

1/2 cup celery, chopped

1 Tomato, diced and seeded

1 1/2 teaspoons sea salt

1/2 teaspoon black pepper

1 teaspoon basil

3 tablespoons soy margarine

3 tablespoons cornstarch, mixed with water to thicken stew

## Directions:

Drain water from the tofu. The best way is to wrap it in plastic wrap and freeze it. Next, allow it to thaw completely. Place the tofu on a dinner plate, and place another dinner plate on top of the tofu. Put something heavy on top of the top plate, such as a few cans or a cast iron skillet. Let the tofu sit for 20 minutes, then drain the water turn the tofu over and repeat.

Once the tofu has been drained, chop it into bite size pieces, then bake on a cookie sheet at 200 degrees. Allow it to bake to dry it out, don't let it turn brown. Usually, about 20 - 30 minutes. Let it bake while you are preparing the rest of the dish by chopping the vegetables.

Add all ingredients, including the baked tofu into the slow cooker. Cook on low for 8 hours, until the vegetables are soft.

Note: Use more cornstarch if needed to thicken the stew. Be sure the cornstarch is completely mixed in with a little water, so that no chunks are present. Once the cornstarch is added into the stew mixture, it takes a little time in the heated slow cooker before you will see it thicken.

# Red Beans and Yams

## Ingredients:

1 onion, chopped

1 can small red beans

2 red bell peppers, chopped

3 cloves of garlic, minced

2 tablespoons fresh ginger, minced

1/2 teaspoon ground cumin

1 can diced tomatoes

3 cups vegetable broth

2 jalapeno peppers, seeded and minced

2 lbs yams, peeled and diced

1/4 teaspoon ground cinnamon

1/2 teaspoon ground coriander

1/2 teaspoon sea salt

1/4 teaspoon ground black pepper

1/4 cup peanuts

1/4 cup peanut butter, creamy not chunky

Optional: lime slices

## Directions:

Add everything except the peanut butter and peanuts into the slow cooker. Stir well to combine, cook on low temperature for 8 hours, until the yams are soft.

Ladle out some of the broth into a small bowl, and mix in the peanut butter. Stir well, to get rid of any peanut butter chunks. Pour the peanut butter mixture back into the slow cooker, stir well and cook for another 20 minutes.

Garnish with the peanuts. Also, fresh lime slices can be used to garnish as well.

# Sundried Tomato and White Bean Stew

## Ingredients:

1 tablespoon extra virgin olive oil

1 red bell pepper, chopped

1 large onion, chopped

1 can diced tomatoes

1/4 cup sun-dried tomatoes

2 cans white beans, drained and rinsed

1 1/2 cups vegetable broth

Dash of salt and ground pepper

1/4 cup of basil pesto sauce

## Directions:

On the stovetop, sauté the onion in the oil for 5 minutes. Add everything except the pesto into the slow cooker.

Cook on low for 6 hours. Before serving, add in the pesto and stir well to mix together.

# Vegan Taco Soup

## Ingredients:

1 onion, chopped

3 cans diced tomatoes with chilies

1 1/2 cups corn

1 can of chopped green chilies (4 ounces)

1 can pinto beans, ranch-style

2 tablespoons powdered vegetable bouillon

1 tablespoon fresh cilantro

1/2 teaspoon chili powder

1/4 teaspoon thyme

1/4 teaspoon cumin

Garnish: cilantro, chopped green onions, and/or tortilla chips

## Directions:

Add all ingredients in the slow cooker, cook for 4 hours on high. Garnish with green onions, cilantro or tortilla chips.

# Barley and Red Beans

## Ingredients:

1 cup uncooked barley

1 celery rib, chopped

1 red onion, chopped

1 clove of garlic, minced

28 ounces of crushed tomatoes (1 large or 2 small cans)

1 can kidney beans, rinsed and drained

1/4 teaspoon red pepper flakes, crushed

3 cups vegetable broth

1 teaspoon salt

2 bay leaves

1/4 teaspoon black pepper

## Directions:

Add everything to the slow cooker, cook on low for 6 hours. Add more vegetable broth if needed.

# Minestrone Soup Mexican-Style

## Ingredients:

2 cups green beans

2 cups red potatoes, diced

1 can garbanzo beans, rinsed and drained

2 cans black beans, rinsed and drained

1 large can stewed tomatoes (or 2 smaller cans)

1 4 ounce can green chilies

1 can corn, drained

1 cup salsa

3 cups vegetable broth

1 tablespoon chili powder

salt and pepper to taste

## Directions:

Add everything to the slow cooker, cook on low for 8 hours. Optional: serve with a garnishment of cilantro or tortilla chips.

# Sweet Potato Risotto

## Ingredients:

1/2 tablespoon extra virgin olive oil

2 large onions

2 garlic cloves, minced

1/2 teaspoon dried rosemary

2 sweet potatoes, peeled and diced

3 cups vegetable broth

1 1/2 cups pearl barley

## Directions:

On the stovetop, sauté the onion in olive oil for 4 minutes, add in the spices and sauté for another minute. Add in the broth and bring to a boil. Pour into the slow cooker.

Combine all ingredients into the slow cooker. Cook on low for 7 hours. The risotto is ready when the potatoes are cooked.

# Couscous Tomato Soup

## Ingredients:

1 tablespoon extra virgin olive oil

1 onion, chopped

1 clove of garlic, minced

1 large can crushed tomatoes (or 2 smaller cans)

3 cups vegetable broth

1 teaspoon sugar

1 tablespoon tomato paste

2 bay leaves

salt and black pepper to taste

1 cup cooked couscous

Garnish: fresh basil leaves

## Directions:

Sautee the onion and garlic in the oil on the stove top for about 5 minutes. Add the onion and garlic into the slow cooker, add all other ingredients except couscous and basil. Cook on low for 8 hours. Remove bay leaves and stir in the couscous. Garnish with fresh basil before serving.

# Coconut Sweet Potato Soup

## Ingredients:

2 teaspoons extra virgin olive oil

1 onion, chopped

3 cloves garlic, minced

2 cups sweet potatoes, diced

1 red bell pepper, chopped

2 jalapenos, seeded and minced

1 1/2 cups red kidney beans

1 can diced tomatoes, drained

1 can coconut milk

1/2 teaspoon thyme

4 cups vegetable broth

1/4 teaspoon allspice, ground

Salt and black pepper to taste

8 ounces fresh spinach

## Directions:

Heat the oil in a skillet, add the onion and garlic and sauté for 5 minutes. Spoon the cooked onion and garlic into the slow cooker. Add the bell pepper, sweet potatoes, jalapeno, beans, and tomatoes. Top the vegetables with the spices, then pour the broth over everything. Stir to mix all of the ingredients together.

Set the slow cooker to a low temperature, cook for 6 hours. It is done when the vegetables are soft. Add in the coconut milk and spinach for the last 30 minutes of cooking.

# Slow Cooker Greens and Beans

## Ingredients:

2 tablespoons extra virgin olive oil

4 garlic cloves, minced

1 cup onion, chopped

1 handful of fresh parsley

4 cups chopped kale or spinach

1 can black beans, rinsed and drained

1/4 teaspoon white pepper

2 teaspoons herbes de Provence

1 cup vegetable broth

## Directions:

In a skillet, sauté the garlic and onion in the olive oil. Cook for 5 minutes, then add to the slow cooker. Add everything else to the slow cooker, stir well. Cook on low for 5 hours.

# Pumpkin Chili

## Ingredients:

1 bag of vegetarian crumbles (ground meat substitute)

1 onion, chopped

1 canned pumpkin puree (canned pumpkin)

1 can kidney beans, rinsed and drained

1 (28 ounce) can diced tomatoes, Italian seasoned

1 (12 ounces) bottle of chili sauce

2 teaspoons pumpkin pie spice

1 tablespoon chili powder

1 teaspoon freshly ground black pepper

1 teaspoons salt

Optional: green onions, non-dairy grated cheese or sour cream

## Directions:

Add everything in the slow cooker, stir well. Cook on low for 4 hours. Garnish with optional toppings.

# Italian Minestrone Soup

## Ingredients:

1 cup carrots, chopped

1 cup onion, chopped

2 cloves garlic, minced

2 celery stalks, chopped

1 can navy beans, rinsed and drained

1 can diced tomatoes (28 oz)

1 sprig of fresh rosemary

3 cups vegetable broth

2 tablespoons fresh basil, chopped

2 bay leaves

1/4 cup fresh Italian parsley, chopped

2 cups fresh spinach

1 zucchini, chopped

2 cups cooked pasta

salt and freshly ground black pepper

Optional: Vegan parmesan cheese to garnish

## Directions:

In a blender, add 1 cup of broth and all of the beans. Puree to a smooth consistency.

In the slow cooker add the pureed beans, salt, pepper, herbs, garlic, onion, celery, carrots, tomatoes, and broth. Stir together, cook on low for 7 hours.

Add in the spinach and zucchini, cook for another 20 - 30 minutes, then add the pasta, cook for an additional 20 minutes. Remove rosemary and bay leaves before serving. Top with vegan parmesan cheese if you would like.

# Chinese Hot Pot

## Ingredients:

1 onion, chopped

2 salks celery, thinly sliced (diagonally)

2 carrots, thinly sliced (diagonally)

2 cloves garlic, minced

1 can sliced water chestnuts, drained

5 1/2 cups vegetable broth

1 teaspoon fresh ginger, minced

1 tablespoon soy sauce

1/4 teaspoon red pepper flakes

1 cup fresh shiitake mushrooms, sliced

3 green onions, chopped

8 ounces extra-firm tofu, drained and diced

1 handful snow peas, trimmed & cut into 1-inch pieces

1/2 teaspoon toasted sesame oil

**Directions:**

Add the red pepper, ginger, garlic, water chestnuts, celery, carrot, and onion in the slow cooker. Set on low and cook for 7 hours.

Add in the mushrooms, tofu, green onions, and snow peas. Drizzle the oil over the top. Cook for another 30 minutes, serve immediately

# Chow Mein

## Ingredients:

1 pound vegetarian "chicken", chopped

1 1/2 cups carrots, chopped

1 1/2 cups celery, chopped

1 can sliced water chestnuts

1 cup vegetable broth

6 green onions, chopped

1/4 teaspoon red pepper flakes

1/3 cup soy sauce

1 1/2 cups bean sprouts

1/2 teaspoon ginger

1/4 cup cornstarch

1/3 cup water

## Directions:

Set aside corn starch and water. Add everything else to the slow cooker. Turn temperature to low, cook for 8 hours.

20 minutes before the slow cooker is done, mix the water and corn starch  together in a small bowl. Mix very well, to get rid of any cornstarch lumps. Slowly stir the mixture into the slow cooker, cook for 20 minutes to let the broth thicken.

# Polenta Casserole

## Ingredients:

1 can cannellini beans, rinsed and drained

1 can navy beans, rinsed and drained

1/4 cup basil pesto

4 garlic cloves, minced

1 onion, chopped

1 1/2 teaspoons Italian seasoning

1 tomato, sliced

1 (16 ounce) package plain polenta, cut into slices

2 cups non-dairy cheese, shredded

1 cup torn radicchio

2 cups fresh spinach

## Directions:

In a mixing bowl, combine the beans, Italian seasoning, garlic, onion and 2 tablespoons pesto.

Layer the casserole in the slow cooker. Add half the bean mixture on the bottom, half of the polenta, and then half of the grated cheese. Repeat to layer again.

Cook on low for 6 hours. Then layer on the tomato, more vegan cheese, radicchio, and spinach. In a small bowl, combine 1 tablespoon water and the rest of the pesto, stir together. Drizzle the pesto mixture over the casserole. Cook for another 10 minutes, then serve.

# Cornmeal Dumpling Stew

## Stew Ingredients:

2 cups fresh mushrooms, sliced

3 cups butternut squash, cubed

1 can Great Northern beans, drained and rinsed

2 cans diced tomatoes, un-drained

4 garlic cloves , minced

1 cup water

1/4 teaspoon freshly ground black pepper

1 teaspoon Italian seasoning

2 cups green beans

## Dumpling Ingredients:

1/3 cup cornmeal

1/2 cup flour

1 tablespoon fresh parsley, chopped

2 tablespoons vegan parmesan cheese

1/4 teaspoon sea salt

1 teaspoon baking powder

2 tablespoons almond milk

1 egg replacer product of your choice

2 tablespoons extra virgin olive oil

## Directions:

Add the beans, tomatoes (and juice from the tomato can), mushrooms, squash, water, Italian seasoning, garlic, and pepper. Stir together and cook on live for 8 hours.

Make the dumpling batter in a mixing bowl. Add the salt, baking powder, parsley, vegan parmesan, cornmeal, and flour. Mix dry ingredients together, then add the oil, milk, egg replacer and flour. Stir with a fork to combine the ingredients.

Turn the slow cooker to high, stir in the green beans. Use a spoon to drop the dumpling sough into the slow cooker. Cook for 45 minutes, keeping the lid in place to allow the dumplings to cook.

# Corn and Green Chile Soup

## Ingredients:

1 tablespoon extra virgin olive oil

1 cup onion, diced

2 jalapenos, seeded and chopped

4 roasted Anaheim chilies seeded and chopped

4 roasted poblano chiles, seeded and chopped

6 cups water

2 tablespoons epazote leaves, finely chopped

3 cups corn

1/2 bunch fresh cilantro, chopped

1/2 teaspoon black pepper

2 teaspoons sea salt

## Directions:

Heat a skillet over medium heat, warm the oil, then add the chilies and onion. Sautee for 4 minutes, then add the onion mixture to the slow cooker.

In a food processor, add the corn and pulse several times to chop. Add the chopped corn into the slow cooker.

In the slow cooker, add in the salt and water. Cook on low for at least 6 hours. Then, add in the black pepper, cilantro and epazote.

Use an immersion blender to blend the vegetables. If you don't have an immersion blender, then the soup can be poured into a blender and blended in batches.

If desired, add more water to thin to desired consistency. Garnish with fresh cilantro before serving.

# Chipotle Barley Soup

## Ingredients:

5 cups white beans (navy, cannellini, and/or great northern)

1 potato, diced

1 cup barley, uncooked

2 celery stalks, diced

2 carrots, diced

10 cups vegetable broth

1 cup mushrooms, sliced

1 tablespoon onion flakes, dried

3 tablespoons fresh parsley, chopped

3 bay leaves

1 tablespoon garlic, minced

2 teaspoons chipotle powder

salt and pepper to taste

## Directions:

Rinse and drain the beans. Add them to the slow cooker, along with the rest of the ingredients. Stir well.

Cook on low for 8 hours. Remove the bay leaves before serving.

# Pumpkin Lasagna

## Ingredients:

1 tablespoon extra virgin olive oil

3 sun-dried tomatoes, chopped

1 package tofu

1 can pumpkin

1/4 cup nutritional yeast

1 tablespoon Italian seasoning

1 teaspoon onion powder

2 cloves garlic, minced

salt and pepper, to taste

1 jar marinara sauce

1 package lasagna noodles

1 can navy beans, rinsed and drained

## Directions:

Add the sundried tomatoes and olive oil to the food processor. Process until it forms a paste. Add the tofu, pumpkin, nutritional yeast, Italian seasoning, onion powder, garlic, salt and pepper. Pulse a few times to mix everything together. If needed, add a little water if the mixture is too thick.

Spray the slow cooker with nonstick cooking spray, then begin to layer the lasagna. Put a little bit of sauce at the bottom, then add a layer of noodles, add some of the tomato mixture, then more sauce and some of the white beans. Repeat two more times, so there are 3 layers total. The top layer should be noodles, covered completely with red sauce.

Cook on low for 4 hours, serve immediately.

## Spicy White Bean Soup

### Ingredients:

1 can navy beans, drained and rinsed

1 can chickpeas, drained and rinsed

2 (4 ounce) cans green chilies

1 can corn, drained and rinsed

2 cloves garlic, chopped

1 onion, chopped

2 zucchini, diced

4 jalapenos, seeded and chopped (may keep some of the seeds if you want spice)

4 cups vegetable broth

1 pound mushrooms, sliced

1 teaspoon cumin

1 teaspoon oregano

1/2 cup uncooked quinoa

Garnish Optional: tortilla chips, lime slices, and/or cilantro

## Directions:

Set the quinoa aside, add everything else into the slow cooker. Cook on low for 7 hours.

Rinse the quinoa well, then add it to the slow cooker. Cook on
low for another hour, or until the quinoa is cooked.

Garnish if desired.

# Mushroom Soup

## Ingredients:

1 onion, chopped

2 tablespoons extra virgin olive oil

4 cups vegetable broth

1 can navy beans, drained and rinsed

2 packages mushrooms, chopped

1/2 a lemon, juiced

2 tablespoons paprika

1 tablespoon fresh dill, minced

salt and pepper

Optional: green onions to garnish

## Directions:

Heat a skillet on the stove top, add the oil and then add the onion and sauté for 5 minutes. Add the mushrooms to the skillet, over and cook for 8 minutes.

Add the mushroom mixture into the slow cooker. Cook on low for 8 hours.

Serve the bowls garnished with green onions if desired.

# Ginger Coconut Soup

## Ingredients:

1 sweet potato, diced

2 pounds carrots, chopped

1 onion, chopped

2 teaspoons curry powder

2 teaspoons ginger paste

1 can coconut milk

4 cups vegetable broth

salt and pepper to taste

## Directions:

Add the broth, ginger paste and curry powder to the slow cooker. Use a whisk to mix well. Add in the rest of the ingredients except the coconut milk and stir well.

Cook on low for 8 hours, or until the vegetables are tender. Blend in batches in the blender, or use an immersion blender in the slow cooker. Stir in the coconut milk, serve immediately.

# 5 Bean Vegan Chili

## Ingredients:

1 can diced tomatoes (28 ounce), don't drain

1 can crushed tomatoes (28 ounce), don't drain

1 can tomato paste (6 ounce)

2 cans black beans

2 cans garbanzo beans

1 can light kidney beans

1 can dark red kidney beans

2 cans green beans

1 can vegan refried beans

1 1/2 teaspoons vegetable bouillon

2 1/2 cups carrots, chopped

1 teaspoon cumin

4 tablespoons chili powder

1/2 teaspoon coriander

1/4 teaspoon cayenne pepper

1/2 teaspoon ground pepper

1 tablespoon oregano

4 ounces chipotle chile in adobo, chopped

Optional: Garnish tortilla chips and/or with non-dairy cheese

## Directions:

Rinse and drain all beans, add them to the slow cooker. Add all other ingredients, stir together.

Cook on low for 5 hours. Garnish as desired, serve immediately.

## Coconut Black Beans

### Ingredients:

3 cups cooked black beans

2 onions, chopped

2 tablespoons coconut oil

1 bell pepper, chopped

4 cloves garlic, minced

1 teaspoon dried thyme

1/2 teaspoon cayenne pepper (or to taste)

1 tablespoon brown sugar

1 sweet potato, diced

2 potatoes, diced

1 cup vegetable broth

2 cans diced tomatoes

1 can coconut milk

3 cups cooked brown rice

## Directions:

In a skillet, heat the coconut oil and then sauté the onion, garlic, bell pepper and spices. Cook for 5 minutes

Add the onion mixture to the slow cooker. Add in the rest of the ingredients except the rice and coconut milk. Cook on high for 3 hours, or until potatoes are tender.

Add in the coconut milk and stir well. Add in the rice, stir to incorporate into the slow cooker. Serve immediately.

# Stove Top Vegan Meals

The stove top is one of the most common tools to prepare a dinner meal, and it is a convenient option. There are many types of meals that can be prepared on the stove top, so this recipe section contains a variety of meals to choose from.

Just like the other sections of this recipe book, the recipes focus on one dish meals, which means that you can prepare one main recipe for the meal without having to worry about side dishes. It is much easier to prepare one recipe, instead of trying to fix several different recipes at the same time!

Stove top recipes are simple, delicious and easy to make. They are a great way to make a hot, hearty, healthy meal.

# Black Beans and Quinoa

## Ingredients:

1 cup quinoa, rinsed

2 garlic cloves, minced

2 cups + 3 tablespoons vegetable broth, divided

1/4 cup fresh lemon juice

1 teaspoon chili powder

1 teaspoon flaxseed, ground

1/2 teaspoon cumin

1/4 teaspoon chipotle seasoning

6 cups kale, finely chopped

1 can black beans, drained and rinsed

1/2 cup grated carrot

1/2 cup corn

1/2 red bell pepper, chopped

1 avocado, pit removed and sliced

Pinch of salt, to taste

## Directions:

In a saucepan, gently heat the garlic and drained quinoa, toast it for a few minutes. Add in the vegetable broth, increase heat to bring to a boil. Once it starts boiling, turn the temperature to medium heat and reduce to simmer. Cover the pan while simmering. Cook for 20 minutes, or until the liquid is absorbed. Remove from heat.

During the time that the quinoa is cooking, mix the dressing. In a mixing bowl, add 2 tablespoons of broth, lemon juice, flax seeds, seasonings and salt. Stir well to incorporate all ingredients.

In a large bowl, place the chopped kale. Pour half of the dressing over the kale, and massage the dressing into the kale with your hands. Stir in the black beans, carrots, bell pepper and quinoa, drizzle the rest of the dressing over the top and stir everything together.

Chill in the fridge for 2 - 3 hours before serving. If needed, add more lemon juice or spice. Garnish with fresh avocado slices.

# Citrus Edamame Quinoa

## Ingredients:

1 tablespoon extra virgin olive oil

1 1/2 cups quinoa, uncooked rinsed well

4 scallions, chopped

6 boy choy stalks, chopped

1 red bell pepper, chopped

1 cup shelled edamame

4 tablespoons soy sauce

1 teaspoon sesame oil

1 teaspoon ginger, grated

1/2 cup cashews, toasted

2 mandarins, peeled and separated

Sea salt and ground black pepper to taste

## Directions:

Cook the quinoa in a saucepan, add it to 3 cups of water and bring to a boil. Simmer for 20 minutes, until the water has been absorbed.

Heat the olive oil in a skillet. Add the bell pepper and edamame, stir fry for a few minutes. Then, add the scallions and bok choy, continue to cook for 2 minutes. The bok choy should be wilted.

Stir the quinoa into the skillet, drizzle the sesame oil over the top. Drizzle the soy sauce, pepper, and ginger. Stir well to incorporate the seasonings. Top with the cashews and oranges, stir gently to combine. Serve immediately.

# Vegetable Miso Soup

## Ingredients:

1/2 teaspoon extra virgin olive oil

4 garlic cloves, minced

1 tablespoon ginger, minced

1/2 tablespoon seaweed

12 cups water

1 1/2 ounces shiitake mushrooms, dried

1 1/2 cups matchstick carrots

1 1/2 cups shelled edamame

1 pound bok choy, chopped into 1/2-inch pieces

5 ounces rice noodles, uncooked

8 tablespoons white vegan miso

Optional: Serve with green onions to garnish the bowls, or wasabi if you want more spice.

## Directions:

In a large pot, heat the oil and sauté the ginger and garlic for 1 -2 minutes. Next, add water, seaweed, carrots, and mushrooms. Bring everything to a simmer. Cover, and simmer for at least 15 - 20 minutes. The mushrooms should be tender.

Next, add edamame and cook for 6 minutes. Add the noodles and bok choy. Cover and simmer until the noodles are tender, about 7 or 8 minutes.

In a small mixing bowl, add the miso and a ladle of broth from the pan. Whisk together well to remove lumps, then pour back into the pot. Heat for 3 or 4 minutes, and then serve hot.

# Pesto Pasta and Broccoli

## Ingredients:

16 ounces spiral pasta

1 broccoli bunch, chopped

1 zucchini, sliced

3 garlic cloves

3 cups basil, fresh

1/8 cup almonds, slivered or sliced

6 ounces tofu

1 can chickpeas

2 tablespoons nutritional yeast

2 teaspoons lemon juice

1 teaspoon sea salt

1 large tomato (or 2 small tomatoes), diced

## Directions:

Fill a large pot and bring it to a boil. Add in the pasta and bring it to a boil again, cook for 7 minutes. Next, add in the broccoli and cook for 4 minutes. Add the zucchini and cook for 1-2 minutes.

Drain the water and run cold water over the pasta and vegetables. Drain well.

Make the dressing in a food processor. Add the garlic, almonds, and nutritional yeast to the processor, plus a few times to chop. Add in the lemon juice, salt, basil, and tofu. Process well until a smooth consistency is achieved.

In a large mixing bowl, combine the pasta and vegetables with the chickpeas, tomato, and stir the pesto sauce in to evenly coat everything. Sprinkle almonds over the top and serve.

# Sweet Potato & Cauliflower Curry Soup

## Ingredients:

1 tablespoon extra virgin olive oil

1 tablespoon ginger, minced

1 onion, chopped

1/2 teaspoon cumin seeds

1 jalapeno pepper, seeded and minced

3 garlic cloves, minced

4 cups vegetable broth

1 large sweet potato, peeled and cubed

1 head cauliflower, chopped

1 tablespoon curry powder, divided

1/8 teaspoon cinnamon

1 can diced tomatoes

1 can chickpeas, rinsed and drained

1 tablespoon peanut butter

3 cups water

1 teaspoon salt

1/4 tsp cayenne pepper

## Directions:

In a big pot, heat the oil and add the onion, garlic, ginger, pepper and cumin. Sautee for a few minutes to soften the onion, then add in the broth, 1 teaspoon curry, cinnamon, and sweet potatoes. Bring it to a boil, lower heat and simmer for 20 minutes, or until the potato is soft.

Add in the chickpeas, cauliflower, and tomatoes, stir everything together. Pour in enough water to cover the vegetables, also add the rest of the curry powder, cayenne, and salt. Cover the pot, simmer for 20 minutes.

In a small bowl, add the peanut butter and a ladle of hot broth. Mix together well to get rid of the peanut butter chunks, then pour into the soup. Stir well.

# Pineapple Thai Rice

## Ingredients:

3 cups cooked brown rice

2 tablespoons olive oil

2 garlic cloves, minced

1 onion, sliced

1 bell pepper, diced

4 scallions, sliced

2 cups broccoli, chopped

2 carrots, sliced

2 tomatoes, diced

2 cups pineapple, chopped

1 cup coconut milk

2 tablespoons soy sauce

2 teaspoons ginger, minced

1 teaspoon curry powder

Garnish: Cashews, peanuts, cilantro, bean sprouts, etc

## Directions:

In a skillet, heat the oil and add the onion and garlic, sauté for 6 or 7 minutes. Add the bell pepper, carrots, and broccoli, sauté for 3 or 4 minutes. Add in the pineapple, tomatoes, and scallions, cook for another 2 minutes.

Add in the rice, ginger, soy sauce, curry powder, and coconut milk. Stir well, to combine all ingredients. Garnish with toppings of choice and serve immediately.

# Cranberry Quinoa

## Ingredients:

1 1/4 cups uncooked quinoa, rinsed well

1 tablespoon extra virgin olive oil

1 head cauliflower, chopped

1 onion, chopped

2 garlic cloves, minced

1/3 cup sliced almonds or pine nuts, toasted

1/2 cup dried cranberries

1 tablespoon flaxseed oil

1/4 cup fresh parsley, minced

Salt and ground pepper

## Directions:

In a saucepan, add the quinoa and 2 1/2 cups of water. Simmer until the quinoa absorbs the water, about 15 minutes.

While the quinoa is cooking, heat the oil in a skillet. Sautee the onion and garlic for a few minutes, until the onion is soft. Add a little bit of water (about 1/4 cup), then add the cauliflower into the skillet. Cover and simmer until the cauliflower is cooked, about 5 minutes.

Add the cooked quinoa to the skillet, as well as the nuts, parsley and cranberries. Stir together and take the skillet off the stove. Drizzle the flax oil over the top, sprinkle on salt and pepper to taste. Serve immediately.

## Avocado Black Bean Wraps

### Ingredients:

4 cups cooked black beans

2 tablespoons extra virgin olive oil

2 garlic cloves, minced

1 bell pepper, chopped

1 can crushed tomatoes, drained

1 (4-ounce) can chopped green chilies

1 teaspoon ground cumin

Pinch of sea salt

1 tomato, finely chopped

1 avocado, sliced or mashed

Salsa

Shredded lettuce

8 corn tortillas

Optional: Grated vegan cheese and/or Vegan sour cream

**Directions:**

In a small bowl, use a fork to mash the beans to a coarse consistency.

In a skillet, heat the olive oil, then add the garlic and pepper. Sautee for 5 -6 minutes. Add in the tomatoes, chilies, seasonings, and beans. Stir to mix all ingredients. Turn heat down to low, cook for 10 minutes.

To assemble the wraps add the bean mixture, top with lettuce, add tomato and avocado, as well as any other desired toppings. Wrap together like a burrito and eat.

# Vegan Minestrone Soup

## Ingredients:

2 tablespoons extra virgin olive oil

2 garlic cloves, minced

1 onion, chopped

3 carrots, sliced

4 celery stalks, chopped

28-ounce can diced tomatoes

4 cups white beans

5 cups water

1 1/2 cups pasta

2 bay leaves

1/4 cup dry red wine

2 teaspoons Italian seasonings

1 teaspoon basil

1/2 cup green peas

Salt and black pepper to taste

Garnish with fresh parsley and/or fresh basil

## Directions:

In a big pot, warm the olive oil. Add the onion and garlic, cook for 5 minutes until soft. Add in the carrots and celery, cook for another few minutes until the carrots are tender.

Add to the pot: herbs, bay leaves, win, water, beans, and tomatoes. Bring the pot to a boil, lower heat, and simmer for 30 minutes.

Cook the pasta according to the directions on the package. Drain and rinse the pasta, then add it to the soup. Add the peas and simmer for 5 minutes. If needed, add more water.

Garnish each soup bowl with parsley and/or basil leaves.

# Southwest Flavored Quinoa

## Ingredients:

1/4 cup fresh lime juice

1 1/2 tablespoons lime zest

6 tablespoons extra virgin olive oil

1/2 tablespoons apple cider vinegar

2 cups uncooked quinoa, rinsed well

1 tablespoons maple syrup

2 cans black beans, drained and rinsed

3 3/4 cups water

8 green onions, finely chopped

3 cups tomatoes, diced

1 cup cilantro, chopped

Sea salt and black pepper, to taste

## Directions:

In a small bowl, add the lime zest, lime juice, olive oil, vinegar, and maple syrup. Whisk together well.

In a saucepan, add the water and quinoa, bring to a boil. Once it starts boiling, reduce heat to simmer for 20 minutes. Use a fork to fluff the quinoa, then add the cilantro, green onions, tomatoes, and black beans. Drizzle the dressing over top. Stir well to combine all ingredients, season with salt and pepper as needed. Serve immediately.

# Basic Stir Fry

## Ingredients:

2 tablespoons extra virgin olive oil

1 onion, chopped

1 zucchini, chopped

1 red bell pepper, chopped

1 cup mushrooms, sliced

2 cups bean sprouts, fresh

1 tablespoon agave

1/3 cup soy sauce

1/2 teaspoon black pepper

8 ounces noodles, cooked

## Directions:

Cook the noodles according to package directions, drain well and set aside in a large bowl.

Warm the olive oil in a pan over medium heat. Add in the onion, and cook for 2 minutes. Then, add the zucchini and sauté for another 3 minutes. Add the onion mixture to the bowl with the noodles.

Add more oil in the skillet if needed, sauté the bell pepper and mushrooms for 2 minutes. Scoop the mushroom mixture into the bowl with the noodles.

If needed, add a little more oil in the skillet, and sauté the bean sprouts in the soy sauce, agave, and black pepper. Sautee for 2 minutes, and then add the rest of noodles and the cooked vegetables that were set aside. Cook for 8 minutes.

Serve immediately.

# Pea and Lima Bean Soup

## Ingredients:

14 cups water

1 1/2 cups carrots, chopped

2 cups onion, chopped

2/3 cups parsley, chopped

2 cups celery, chopped

2 cloves garlic, minced

4 green onions, chopped

2/3 cups dried green split peas

1 zucchini, diced

1 cup lima beans

2 tablespoons barley

1 tablespoon vegetable bouillon

Salt and freshly ground pepper to taste

## Directions:

In a large stock pot, add the water and turn heat on high to bring to a boil. Then, add in all of the ingredients and bring it back to a boil.

Reduce heat to low, simmer for 40 minutes. You will see foam forming on top of the soup, use a spoon to scoop off the foam until it stops forming.

After 40 minutes, the foam should be done. Cover the pot with a lid, continue simmering for 2 hours.

Before serving, add salt and pepper to taste. If needed, add more bouillon for flavor.

# Tomato and Quinoa Wraps

## Ingredients:

2 wraps (10-inches in size)

1 cup cooked quinoa

1/4 cup green onion, chopped

3/4 cup hummus

1 tomato, chopped

6 sun-dried tomatoes, chopped

Mixed greens of your choice

## Directions:

Cook the quinoa on the stove top, according to the directions on the package.

To assemble the wraps, spread hummus on the wrap, then add quinoa on top and layer on all other ingredients. Fold the wrap tightly and eat immediately.

# Bok Choy Tofu Stir Fry

## Ingredients:

1 package firm tofu

2 tablespoons extra virgin olive oil

1 onion, thinly sliced

1 bell pepper, chopped

Bok choy, chopped

3 tablespoons soy sauce

2 teaspoons ginger, grated

1/4 cup almonds, slivered or sliced

## Directions:

Prepare the tofu by cutting it into slices. Blot between a few paper towels to remove excess moisture. Cut into bite-size pieces.

In a skillet, heat the olive oil over medium heat, add the tofu and stir fry until the tofu has a nice golden color. Remove the tofu from the pan.
In the same skillet, add the onion and sauté for about 5 minutes, until the onion is soft. Then, add in the bell pepper and continue cooking for another 5 minutes. Add in the ginger and bok choy, stir fry until the bok choy begins to wilt.

Add the tofu back into the skillet. Drizzle the soy sauce over top, stir to combine. Serve immediately. Garnish each serving with the almonds.

# Home-Style Skillet

## Ingredients:

8 ounces red potatoes, diced and cooked until tender

2 tablespoons extra virgin olive oil, divided

1/2 bell pepper, chopped

1/2 onion, chopped

2 garlic cloves, minced

1 package extra-firm tofu, pressed to remove moisture, diced

4 cups Swiss chard, stems removed, chopped

1 lemon, juiced

1 cup mushrooms, sliced

3 tablespoons nutritional yeast

1 teaspoon dried parsley

1 teaspoon dried basil

1/2 teaspoon turmeric

1 teaspoon dried thyme

Pinch cayenne pepper

1 teaspoon salt, to taste

6 ounces vegan sausage (optional)

## Directions:

Cook the potatoes according to your preference (boil, steam, bake, or microwave). The potatoes should be firm enough to not fall apart, but tender enough to pierce with a fork.

In a skillet, turn on the burner to medium-high and heat a tablespoon of olive oil. Add the potatoes to the skillet, and cook for 8 minutes. The potatoes should start turning brown. When the potatoes are brown, remove from the skillet and set aside.

Next, add another tablespoon of oil to the skillet, and cook the onions for 3 minutes. Add in the pepper and sausage (if you choose to use vegan sausage), and cook for another 3 minutes. Add in the mushrooms, chard, and tofu. Stir regularly and cook for 5 minutes.

Add the cayenne, salt, herbs, lemon juice, and nutritional yeast. Cook for another 5 minutes, adding a tiny amount of water if the pan is too dry. Add the potatoes back into the skillet, cook for 5 more minutes and then serve.

# Sweet Potato Chili

## Ingredients:

3 sweet potatoes, skinned and diced

1 red bell pepper, diced

2 tablespoons extra virgin olive oil

3 garlic cloves, minced

1 cup onion, chopped

4 cans black beans, rinsed and drained

1 can corn

One can diced tomatoes (28-ounce)

One can crushed tomatoes (16-ounce)

8 ounces chopped mild green chiles (2 4-ounce cans)

1 teaspoon dried oregano

2 teaspoons cumin, ground

1/4 cup fresh parsley, minced

1/4 cup fresh cilantro, minced

Salt and black pepper

## Directions:

Cook the sweet potatoes until they are firm, but just starting to soften. You can boil, bake or microwave them. Set the sweet potatoes to the side.

In a large pot, heat the olive oil, add in the garlic and onion and sauté until the onion is soft. Add everything else into the pot, except the sweet potato, parsley, salt and pepper. Stir well, and simmer for 15 minutes.

Next, add in the diced sweet potatoes, stir well and simmer for 15 minutes. Continue simmering until all of the veggies are soft.

Before serving, stir in the cilantro and parsley. Add salt and pepper as needed.

# White Bean Rotini

## Ingredients:

8 ounces uncooked rotini pasta

2 tablespoon extra virgin olive oil

2 garlic cloves, minced

1/2 cup onion, chopped

1 red bell pepper, chopped

1 can Italian-style diced tomatoes, do not drain

1 can cannellini beans, rinsed and drained

1/3 cup raisins

1/4 cup sun-dried tomatoes, chopped

1/2 teaspoon red pepper flakes

8 ounces baby spinach, fresh

1 teaspoon dried oregano

Salt and pepper

## Directions:

Cook pasta according to directions on the package. Drain well after cooking.

In a skillet, heat the oil and then sauté the bell pepper, garlic and onion. Cook for 5 minutes, then add the canned tomatoes, beans, sundried tomatoes, red pepper flakes, raisins, and oregano. Bring to a simmer, cover the pan, simmer for 6 minutes.

Add in the spinach and stir it into the mixture. Cook until the spinach wilts.

In a large mixing bowl, add the pasta and the tomato mixture. Toss together, add a little salt and pepper if desired. Serve immediately.

# Tofu and Broccoli Stir Fry

## Stir Fry Ingredients:

1 package firm tofu, drained well to removed excess water and diced

1/2 cup vegetable broth

1 tablespoon peanut oil

1 cup onion, sliced

2 bell peppers, sliced

6 cups broccoli, chopped

Optional: chopped peanuts, green onions, bean sprouts

8 ounces rice noodles

## Sauce Ingredients:

2 cloves garlic, minced

1 teaspoon peanut oil

1 tablespoon Braggs Liquid Aminos

1 cup vegetable broth

1 tablespoon minced ginger, fresh

1 teaspoon garlic chile paste

1 tablespoon vegan Worcestershire sauce

1/4 cup rice vinegar

1 1/2 tablespoons cornstarch

## Directions:

Follow the rice noodle package directions to cook. Set the noodles to the side,

In a small bowl, add all of the sauce ingredients and whisk well.

In a skillet, heat the peanut oil on medium high heat. Add in the tofu, and brown the tofu. Take the tofu out of the pan, set aside.

In the skillet, add the broccoli and vegetable broth. Cook until the broccoli is just tender, about 10 minutes. Next, add the tofu and noodles to the skillet, drizzle the sauce over the top. Cook for about 5 minutes to heat everything, stir well to evenly coat everything in the sauce.

Garnish with peanuts, bean sprouts, and/or green onions.

# Sweet Potato Ravioli

## Ingredients:

1 tablespoon extra virgin olive oil

2 garlic cloves, minced

1 onion, chopped

2 1/2 cups sweet potato, diced

1 cup almond milk

1/2 teaspoon salt

1 package vegan ravioli (with tofu or vegetable filling)

## Directions:

In a saucepan, heat the olive oil then add the garlic and onion. Sautee until the onion is well-cooked, about 6 minutes. Add the sweet potato, add enough water to cover the potato completely. Cover, and simmer for 15 - 20 minutes. The potatoes should be tender.

Put the sweet potatoes and onion into a food processor, also add the salt and almond milk. Run the processor until everything is a smooth consistency. Put the sweet potato mixture back into the skillet.

Cook the ravioli according to the directions on the package. Drain the ravioli, then add them to the skillet with the sweet potato mixture. Heat on low heat, then serve immediately.

# Sundried Tomatoes and Bow Tie Pasta

## Ingredients:

12 ounces bowtie pasta, uncooked

2 cups cannellini beans

8 ounces mushrooms, sliced

1 1/2 tablespoons extra virgin olive oil

4 garlic cloves, minced

3/4 cup almond milk

1/4 cup dry white wine

1/2 cup sun-dried tomatoes, chopped

Salt and pepper to taste

Optional: Vegan Parmesan cheese

## Directions:

Cook pasta according to the directions on the package. Rinse well and drain.

In a food processor, add the rice milk and beans. Process to achieve a smooth consistency. Set aside for a moment.

In a saucepan, heat the olive oil and the add the garlic and sauté for 2 minutes. Add in the mushrooms and wine, continue cooking on medium heat for 5 or 6 minutes. Next, add in the bean puree and sundried tomatoes. Bring the mixture to a simmer, then cook for another 6 minutes.

In a large mixing bowl, add the pasta and top with mushroom sauce. Toss well to evenly coat the noodles with sauce. Season with salt and pepper as desired. Top with vegan parmesan cheese.

# Pad Thai

## Ingredients:

8 ounces uncooked rice noodles

1 1/2 tablespoons peanut oil

8 ounces firm tofu, pressed to remove excess moisture and chopped

4 garlic cloves, minced

8 ounces bean sprouts, fresh

6 scallions, chopped

1/2 teaspoon Thai red chili paste

1/2 cup fresh cilantro, chopped

1/2 cup peanuts, chopped

Garnish with lime wedges

Optional garnish: sriracha sauce

## Sauce Ingredients:

1 can coconut milk

1/4 cup ketchup

2 tablespoons brown sugar

1 lime, juiced

3 tablespoons soy sauce

## Directions:

Whisk the sauce ingredients together, set aside.

Cook the rice noodles by following the instructions on the package.

In a skillet, heat the oil and then add the garlic and tofu. Stir fry until the tofu is golden brown. Add in the chili paste, scallions, and sprouts. Cover the skillet, cook for 2 - 3 minutes.

Add the cooked noodles into the skillet, pour the sauce over the top and stir to evenly mix everything.

When serving, garnish each plate with fresh lime wedges, peanuts and cilantro.

# Corn Chowder

## Ingredients:

1 package silken tofu

2 tablespoons extra virgin olive oil

1 onion, chopped

2 celery stalks, chopped

2 carrots, sliced

3 cups corn kernels

2 potatoes, diced

2 cubes vegetable bouillon

1/2 teaspoon ground cumin

Almond milk, to achieve desired consistency

Salt and pepper, to taste

## Directions:

In a big pot, heat the oil, turn the temperature to medium heat. Add the celery and onion, sauté for 6 minutes. Next, add in the cumin, bouillon, potatoes, and carrots. Put enough water in the pot to cover the vegetables. Bring to a boil, turn down the heat and simmer for 25 minutes, or until the vegetables are soft.

While the vegetables are cooking, puree the tofu in a blender or food processor. Once the vegetables are cooked, pour the blended tofu into the pot. Stir in the corn. Use almond milk to thin the soup, if needed.

Add a dash of salt and pepper, stir well. Cook for 10 minutes on low.

# Fried Rice

## Ingredients:

1/3 cup extra virgin olive oil

1 onion, diced

3 green onions, chopped

3 garlic cloves, minced

1 1/2-inch ginger piece, peeled and minced

4 cups cooked rice

1/2 cup corn

1/2 cup peas

1/2 cup carrots, chopped

1/2 cup celery, chopped

1/4 cup soy sauce

Salt and pepper

Optional: vegan egg replacer

## Directions:

Using high heat, warm the oil in a skillet, add the onions and sauté for 2 minutes. Add in the green onions, ginger, and garlic and cook for another 1 minute. Add the rest of the vegetables, continue cooking for 7 - 8 minutes.

Optional: If you are using egg replacer, at this point empty the contents of the skillet into a mixing bowl and cook the eggs in the skillet. Once the eggs are cooked, add them to the mixing bowl with the vegetables.

Add 2 tablespoons of oil to the skillet, then add the rice. Sautee for 4 -5 minutes, stirring well to break up rice clumps that may be present. Add the vegetable mixture, pour the soy sauce over the top, and sauté for 2 - 3 minutes until everything is warmed through. Add salt and pepper to taste, and more soy sauce if desired.

# Sweet Pistachio Couscous

## Ingredients:

1 lemon, juiced

1/2 cup red onion, chopped

2 tablespoons extra virgin olive oil, divided

1 1/3 cups dry couscous

2 cups water

1/2 cup shelled pistachios

1 teaspoon sea salt

1/3 cup parsley, chopped

10 dried apricots, chopped

## Directions:

In a small bowl, add the chopped onions and pour the lemon juice over top. Set aside, letting the onions marinate in the lemon juice.

In a saucepan, bring the water to a boil. Add the salt and 1 tablespoon of olive oil, then stir in the couscous. Stir well, remove from heat and cover the pan.

After 6 minutes, move the couscous from the pan into a large mixing bowl. Add the apricots, pistachios, and parsley. Pour the lemon juice and onions over the top and drizzle the second tablespoon of olive oil over the top. Stir well to combine everything. Serve immediately.

# Potato and Pea Soup

## Ingredients:

3 tablespoon extra virgin olive oil

1 onion, chopped

2 cloves garlic, minced

1 can peas, drained

1 celery stalk, chopped

3 carrots, chopped

3 cups vegetable broth

3 potatoes, peeled and diced

1 bay leaf

1/2 teaspoon freshly ground pepper

1/2 teaspoon sea salt

## Directions:

In a large pot, heat the oil over medium heat. Sautee for 4 minutes, then add the carrots, garlic, broth, peas, celery and bay leaf.

Bring to a boil, cover the pot, and simmer for 1 hour. After an hour, add the potatoes and cook another 20 minutes, or until the potatoes are tender.

If the soup is too thick, add more broth or water.

## Baja Beans and Rice

### Ingredients:

3 cups cooked brown rice

1 can corn, drained

1 can black beans, drained and rinsed

1/2 cup red onion, chopped

4 tomatoes, diced

1 jalapeno pepper, seeded and minced

1/2 cup fresh cilantro, chopped

1 tablespoon extra virgin olive oil

1 lime, juiced

1/4 teaspoon freshly ground black pepper

1/2 teaspoon sea salt

A splash of hot sauce

## Directions:

In a mixing bowl, add the rice, jalapeno, cilantro, onion, tomatoes, corn and black beans.

Pour over the top the oil, lime juice, salt, pepper and hot sauce. Stir well to mix everything together.

# Broccoli in Peanut Sauce

## Ingredients:

1 bunch broccoli, chopped

1 package firm tofu, drained and diced

3 tablespoons extra virgin olive oil

2 cups onions, chopped

8 garlic cloves, minced

1 cup peanuts, chopped

1/2 teaspoon sea salt

3 tablespoons tamari

Optional: brown rice

## Sauce Ingredients:

1/2 cup hot water

1/2 cup peanut butter

2 tablespoons tamari

1/4 cup apple cider vinegar

1/2 teaspoon cayenne pepper

2 tablespoons molasses

## Directions:

Prepare the sauce in a small bowl, add all ingredients and whisk well. Set aside.

In a large skillet, heat the olive oil and add the onion and garlic. Sautee for 2 minutes, then add the tofu. Turn the burner to medium hot and cook for 8 minutes, until the tofu starts to brown a little bit.

Add the broccoli, tamari, and peanuts, pour the sauce over the top of the stir fry, and cook for 3 or 4 minutes until the broccoli is tender. Toss well to coat everything in the sauce.

Serve immediately. If desired, serve over brown rice.

# Cilantro Potato Soup

## Ingredients:

1 tomato, seeded and chopped

1 onion, chopped

3 potatoes, peeled and diced

2 garlic cloves, finely minced

1 bunch fresh cilantro, divided

1 cup cooked rice

2 teaspoon vegan bouillon

1 bell pepper, chopped

1/2 teaspoon paprika

1 pinch sea salt

2 tablespoons extra virgin olive oil

1 1/2 quarts water

## Directions:

In a large pot, heat the olive oil and sauté the paprika, potatoes, garlic, and onion for 5 minute.

Tie 2/3 of the cilantro tightly to keep it in a bunch. Add the cilantro bunch, bell pepper, and bouillon to the pot. Add enough water to completely cover all of the vegetables, with an extra 2 inches of water above the vegetables.

Turn the heat on high, and bring it to a boil. Reduce heat, simmer for 20 minutes. Add the rice, and simmer for another 10 minutes.

Remove the cilantro bunch, add in the rest of the cilantro (chopped). Serve immediately.

# Black Bean and Artichoke Wraps

## Ingredients:

1 tablespoon extra virgin olive oil

1 can black beans, drained and rinsed

1 can marinated artichoke hearts (10 ounces), chopped

3 garlic cloves, minced

1 onion, diced

Diced tomatoes

Shredded lettuce

Whole wheat tortillas

## Directions:

In a skillet, heat the oil and sauté the  onion and garlic for 2 minutes. Add in the beans, artichoke hearts, and 1/2 cup water.

Cook on medium heat for 20 minutes. The beans will begin to have a "refried" consistency. Add more water if needed. Assemble the wraps by layering the beans, lettuce, and tomatoes in the whole wheat tortillas.

# Vegetable Cashew Noodles

## Ingredients:

3 tablespoons extra virgin olive oil

1/2 cup onion, thinly sliced

2 teaspoon ginger, grated

4 cloves garlic, minced

1/2 teaspoon chili paste

1 bell pepper, thinly sliced

8 ounces mushrooms, thinly sliced

8 ounces sugar snap peas, sliced in half

1/2 cup water

2 tablespoons seasoned rice vinegar

2 tablespoons soy sauce

1 pound whole wheat noodles, cooked

1/3 cup cashews, chopped

## Directions:

Cook the noodles following the directions on the package. Drain and set aside.

In a skillet, heat the oil and then add in the ginger, garlic, onion and chili paste. Cook for 1 minute, then add in the bell pepper and mushrooms. Sautee for 4 minutes.

Add in the soy sauce, vinegar, and noodles. Toss well to coat the noodles in the sauce. Add more soy sauce if needed. Sautee for 1 minute, and then serve immediately.

When serving, garnish each portion with cashews.

# Oven Baked Vegan Meals

Casseroles and baked dishes are often thought of as "comfort food," and it is common for a person to miss the home-cookin' feeling that a good casserole can offer. But, just because meat is eliminated from your menu, doesn't mean that casseroles and oven dishes are no longer an option. There are many tasty dishes that can be baked in the oven.

The advantage of oven baked meals is the fact that if you are busy, then the casserole dish can often be prepared in advance and stored in the fridge until you are ready to bake it. There are been times when I have prepared the meal the previous day, and it made meal time easy and painless. I simply had to turn on the oven and put in the prepared casserole, and dinner was ready within an hour!

# Chickpea Coconut Curry Casserole

## Ingredients:

1 can chickpeas

1 sweet potato, diced

3/4 cup coconut milk

1 cup water

1 apple, cored and diced

3/4 cup red onion, chopped

2 cloves of garlic, minced

1/4 teaspoon ginger, finely shredded

3/4 teaspoon sea salt

1 teaspoon cumin

1 tablespoon curry powder

1/2 teaspoon turmeric

1 teaspoon dried mustard

1/8 teaspoon allspice

## Directions:

Preheat the oven to 375 degrees. Add everything into a casserole dish, cover tightly with foil.

Bake for 65 minutes, stirring occasionally.

Optional: Split the cooked casserole into 1/4 and 3/4 sections. Puree 3/4 with a hand blender, and combine with the remaining 1/4 before serving.

# Pesto Roasted Vegetables and Pasta

## Ingredients:

1 eggplant, cubed

2 zucchini, diced

1 red onion, chopped

1 red bell pepper, chopped

2 garlic cloves, minced

8 ounces grape tomatoes

8 ounces mushrooms, quartered

16 ounces pasta, spiral is best

1 can chickpeas, rinsed and drained

2 cups basil, fresh

1/4 cup kalamata olives, sliced

2 tablespoons walnuts, chopped

3/4 cup vinaigrette dressing

Salt and black pepper, to taste

## Directions:

Heat the oven to 425 degrees. On a cookie sheet, arrange the zucchini and eggplant. Bake for 15 minutes, and then add the mushrooms, tomatoes, and bell pepper. Sprinkle the as salt and pepper on the top. Bake for another 10 minutes, then remove from the oven.

Cook the pasta according to package directions. Drain well. Add the pasta, olives, chickpeas, and vegetables into a large mixing bowl.

Make the dressing in the food processor. Add the garlic, basil, and walnuts and pulse a few times to chop. Add the vinaigrette to the food processor, and blend until it is smooth and mixed well.

Add the dressing on top of the pasta and vegetables, mix everything together to evening coat in pesto. Can be served warm or chilled.

# Roasted Asparagus and Red Potatoes

## Ingredients:

4 red potatoes, cooked and diced

1 bunch asparagus, chopped into bite size pieces

1 cup chickpeas

3 garlic cloves, unpeeled

1 onion, wedged

1/4 cup balsamic vinaigrette

Salt and black pepper, to taste

## Directions:

Heat the oven to 425 degrees. Cook the potatoes any way (boil, bake, or microwave), potatoes should be cooked but maintain a firm texture.

In a large mixing bowl, add the potatoes and chickpeas.

Spread the asparagus bites and onion wedges on a cookie sheet, put the unpeeled garlic in the corner of the cookie sheet. Bake for 15 minutes, stir halfway through.

Add the asparagus to the mixing bowl. Peel the garlic, and mince it, then add it to the mixing bowl.

Pour the dressing over the top of the potatoes and asparagus, along with salt and pepper. Gently stir to spread the garlic throughout the dish and evenly coat everything with the dressing.

# Vegan Lasagna

## Ingredients:

1 package lasagna noodles

2 jars red pasta sauce

2 packages firm tofu, drained

1 package of frozen spinach, thawed and drained

1/4 cup basil, chopped

2/3 cup nutritional yeast

10 garlic cloves, minced

3 tablespoons miso paste

2 tablespoons lemon juice

## Directions:

Heat the oven to 350 degrees. Cook the lasagna noodles according to the directions on the package.

Crumble to tofu and add it to a mixing bowl, along with the basil, spinach, garlic, nutritional yeast, and lemon. Stir everything together.

Spray a casserole pan with nonstick cooking spray, then begin layering the lasagna. Pour a little bit of red sauce in the pan, layer on 3 of the noodles, then add the tofu mixture. Continue layering in that order until the casserole dish is filled. Finish the top layer with noodles, and enough sauce to cover the noodles. The tofu mixture makes a nice garnish on top.

Bake for 35 minutes, then let it sit for 10 minutes before cutting and serving.

Note: For best results, the spinach should be drained very well. Drain it, and then use your hands to squeeze out excess water.

# Enchilada Casserole

## Ingredients:

8 ounces uncooked pasta

1 red onion, chopped

1 teaspoon extra virgin olive oil

3 bell peppers, seeded and chopped

1 jalapeno pepper, seeded and chopped

2 tablespoons taco seasoning mix, or more if desired

1 can enchilada sauce

1 can black beans, drained and rinsed

1 cup green onions, chopped

1/3-1/2 cup non-dairy cheese

salt and black pepper, to taste

1 - 2 cups crushed tortilla chips, crushed

Garnish options: Avocado, non-dairy sour cream, olives, salsa, chopped tomatoes, etc.

## Directions:

Cook pasta in boiling water for about 7 minutes. The paste should be slightly undercooked, it will cook more in the casserole. Drain pasta and immediately rinse in cold water to cool.

Preheat oven to 350 degrees.

In a skillet, cook the onion, bell peppers, jalapeno in olive oil. Sautee for 5 minutes. Add in the black beans, taco seasoning, and 1/2 of the enchilada sauce. Cook for 5 minutes.

Next, add the pasta, cheese, and green onion to the skillet. Stir well.

In a casserole dish, coat the bottom of the dish with enchilada sauce. Scoop in the enchilada mixture and spread evenly. Top with the rest of the enchilada sauce, and sprinkle with a little bit of cheese.

Bake for 20 minutes. Remove from the oven and let it sit for 5 minutes before serving. Garnish with tortilla chips, or any other desired toppings.

# Roasted Vegetables and Potatoes

## Ingredients:

6 garlic cloves

Pinch of sea salt

2 teaspoons paprika

1/4 teaspoon cayenne pepper

1/2 teaspoon cumin, ground

3/4 cup fresh parsley, chopped

3/4 cup fresh cilantro, chopped

1 lemon, juiced

3 tablespoons + 2 tablespoons extra virgin olive oil, divided

3 tablespoons red wine vinegar

1 1/2 pounds red potatoes, sliced

3 bell peppers (red, yellow, green), sliced

4 celery stalks, chopped into big pieces

1 pound tomatoes, wedged

**Directions:**

Heat the oven to 350 degrees.

In a food processor, add 1/2 teaspoon salt, garlic, cumin, paprika, and cayenne. Process to create a paste, then add the herbs and pulse several times. Next, add the vinegar, lemon juice, and 3 tablespoons olive oil. Run the food processor to blend all the ingredients together.

In a large mixing bowl, add the celery, peppers, and potatoes. Pour the sauce over the top and toss to evenly coat. Spread the potato mixture evenly in a casserole dish. Spread the tomatoes on top, then drizzle with 2 tablespoons of olive oil and sprinkle salt over the whole casserole.

Cover with foil and bake for 35 minutes. After 35 minutes, take off the foil and continue baking for another 25 minutes, or until the vegetables are soft. Serve immediately.

# Roasted Eggplant and Veggies

## Ingredients:

1 large eggplant, chopped

2 pounds potatoes, chopped

3 bell peppers, chopped

1 large onion, chopped

2 zucchini, chopped

3 tomatoes, chopped

1/2 pound fresh mushrooms, sliced

1/2 pound fresh green beans

6 cloves garlic, peeled

1/4 cup fresh oregano, chopped

1/4 cup fresh dill weed, chopped

1/4 cup fresh basil, chopped

3/4 cup extra virgin olive oil

1 can tomato sauce (15 ounces)

salt and pepper to taste

Pita bread

## Directions:

Eggplant should be prepared in advance. Cut into chunks, then soak in salt water for 3 hours to remove bitter taste. Rinse well and drain.

Heat the oven to 375 degrees.

Chop all vegetables into chunks, about 2-inches. Mix all vegetables, including eggplant, with basil, oregano, and dill. Put into a casserole dish, drizzle the tomato sauce and olive oil over the top.

Bake for 1 hour. Remove from the oven, stir the vegetables, add a little water to the casserole dish to maintain moistness, then bake for another 60 - 90 minutes until vegetables are tender.

Serve on pita bread.

# Spinach and Black-Eyed Peas

## Ingredients:

2 cups cooked black-eyed peas

1 onion, chopped

1/4 cup extra virgin olive oil

1 large can diced tomatoes (or 2 small cans, 28 ounces total)

3 cups baby spinach

2 teaspoons sea salt

1 teaspoon ground fennel

## Directions:

Heat oven to 350 degrees.

In a skillet, heat the oil and sauté the spinach, onion, tomatoes, fennel and salt. Sautee on low for 15 minutes.

In a casserole dish, add the beans and onion mixture, stir together. Bake for 15 minutes.

## Garbanzo Bean Pasta

### Ingredients:

1 package spiral pasta (16 ounces)

2 tablespoons extra virgin olive oil

1 onion, diced

3 garlic cloves, minced

1 red bell pepper, chopped

1 green bell pepper, chopped

1 jalapeno pepper, minced

1 can diced tomatoes, juiced included

1 can garbanzo beans, rinsed and drained

1 teaspoon oregano

1 teaspoon basil

1 teaspoon cumin, ground

1 teaspoon paprika, ground

1 teaspoon coriander, ground

salt and black pepper

Optional: non-dairy cheese for the top

## Directions:

Heat the oven to 350 degrees. Cook pasta for 7 minutes. Pasta should be undercooked, it will continue cooking in the oven.

In a skillet, heat the olive oil and sauté the onion, bell peppers, jalapeno, and garlic. Sautee for 5 minutes. Add in the garbanzo beans, tomatoes and seasonings. Simmer for 5 minutes, then stir in the pasta.

Spray nonstick cooking spray in a casserole dish. Pour the pasta mixture into the casserole dish, top with non-dairy cheese if desired. Bake for 30 minutes. Let it sit for 10 minutes before serving.

## Rosemary Root Vegetables

### Ingredients:

1 cup red potatoes, cubed

1 yam, cubed

1 jicama, chopped

4 carrots, chopped

2 turnips, chopped

1 parsnip, chopped

6 garlic cloves, minced

1/4 cup fresh rosemary, minced

5 tablespoons olive oil

1 tablespoon sea salt

### Directions:

Heat the oven to 400 degrees.

Prep the vegetables by washing, peeling, and chopping everything, In a large mixing bowl, combine all vegetables. Sprinkle rosemary, garlic, and salt over the top. Drizzle the olive oil over the top. Toss to evenly coat the vegetables.

Put the vegetables in a casserole dish, and bake for 45 minutes, the vegetables should be tender.

# Shepherd's Pie

## Mashed Potato Ingredients:

3 lb. red potatoes, peeled and chopped

1/3 cup + 2 tablespoons almond milk, divided

2 tablespoons nondairy margarine

1 teaspoon sea salt

1/2 teaspoon garlic powder

Freshly ground black pepper, to taste

1 packet vegan gravy mix

## Filling Ingredients:

2 tablespoon extra virgin olive oil

3 garlic cloves, minced

1 onion, chopped

2 parsnips, diced

4 carrots, diced

4 celery stalks, diced

1 - 1 1/2 cups vegetable broth

2 teaspoon dried thyme

1/2 teaspoon Italian seasoning

3/4 teaspoon sea salt

Pinch of black pepper

3 tablespoons whole wheat flour

## Directions:

Cook the potatoes on the stovetop by boiling in water for at least 30 minutes, or until a tender consistency is achieved. When the potatoes are done, drain the water and mash with the almond milk, mashed potato seasonings, and vegan margarine spread.

Preheat the oven to 425 degrees. In a skillet, heat the olive oil and sauté garlic and onions for 5 minutes. Add the celery, carrots, and parsnips. Cook on for 15 minutes on medium-low heat.

Whisk together the broth, flour, salt, pepper, and thyme. Add the liquid to the skillet. Cook until it thickens, about 10 minutes.

Spray the vegetable dish with non-stick cooking spray. Put the vegetable mixture into the dish, spread evenly. Top with the mashed potatoes, spread evenly. Garnish with a little bit of paprika, thyme and freshly ground pepper.

Bake for 35 minutes, then take the casserole out of the oven and let it cool for 10 minutes.

While the casserole is cooking, make the vegan gravy by following the instructions on the packet. Gravy can be served on the side, or drizzled over the top of the potatoes before serving.

# Mac N' Cheeze With Butternut Squash

## Ingredients:

3 1/2 cups butternut squash, chopped

1 cup almond milk

3/4 cup cashews

7 tablespoons Nutritional yeast

3 garlic cloves

1 tablespoon lemon juice

2 teaspoon sea salt

1/2 teaspoon Italian seasoning

1/2 teaspoon paprika

1/2 tsp dijon mustard

1/4 tsp tumeric powder

Freshly ground black pepper

4 1/2 cups dry pasta

Optional: breadcrumbs

## Directions:

Preheat the oven to 350 degrees. On a baking sheet, add the butternut squash lightly coated with a little bit of olive oil and sprinkle sea salt on the top. Bake for 20 minutes, turn the squash pieces over and bake for another 20 minutes.

Cook the pasta according to the package instructions. Don't over-cook, because overcooked noodles will get soggy in the casserole dish. Rinse the pasta in cold water, and drain well.

Make the cheeze sauce in a food processor. Add the seasonings, nutritional yeast, lemon, garlic, milk, and cashews. Process well to mix everything together.

When the squash is done, add it to the food processor with the cheeze mixture and turn it on again until you get a smooth consistency. If needed, add more milk to thin.

Combine pasta and cheezy sauce, stir to evenly coat. Put it in a casserole dish, top with bread crumbs. Bake for 20 minutes, let it sit for 5 minutes before serving.

# Cheezy Green Chile Rice

## Ingredients:

4 cups cooked brown rice

8 ounces nondairy cheese, grated

1 tablespoon extra virgin olive oil

1 onion, chopped

2 garlic cloves, minced

2 (4-ounce) cans mild green chilies, chopped

1 cup vegan sour cream

1/4 cup fresh cilantro, chopped

1/2 teaspoon cumin, ground

Salt and black pepper to taste

## Directions:

Heat the oven to 350 degrees.

In a skillet, heat the olive oil and add the onion and garlic. Sautee for 6 - 8 minutes.

In a large mixing bowl, add all of the ingredients including the cooked onions. Stir together well.

Spray a casserole dish with nonstick cooking spray, then put the rice mixture into the casserole dish. Bake until the top is golden, about 35 minutes.

# Southwestern Zucchini Casserole

## Ingredients:

2 tablespoons extra virgin olive oil

1 cup onion, chopped

1 (4-ounce) can chopped mild green chiles

28-ounce can crushed tomatoes

1 can black beans, rinsed and drained

1 green bell pepper, chopped

2 teaspoons chili powder

1 teaspoon cumin, ground

1 teaspoon dried oregano

1 zucchini, sliced

8 ounces cheddar-style nondairy cheese

12 corn tortillas

**Directions:**

Preheat the oven to 400 degrees.

In a saucepan, heat the oil and cook the onion and bell peppers until soft. Add the seasonings, tomatoes, zucchini and beans. Simmer on medium-low heat for 5 minutes.

Prepare a casserole dish by spraying it with non-stick cooking spray. Layer the casserole with half of the tortillas (tear the tortillas to shape them so that they fill the bottom of the dish). On top of the tortillas, layer half of the bean mixture, then a layer of cheese. Next, put another layer of tortillas, and then finish with a second layer of the bean mixture. Top it off with the cheese.

Bake for 20 minutes, then allow it to cool for 10 minutes before serving.

# Vegetable Pot Pie

## Ingredients:

8 potatoes, diced

2 tablespoons extra virgin olive oil

1 onion, chopped

3 cups diced vegetables(such as broccoli, cauliflower, peas, carrots, corn kernels, yellow squash, zucchini, mushrooms, greens, etc.)

1 cup vegetable broth

2 tablespoons unbleached white flour

1 1/2 tablespoons Mrs. Dash seasoning blend

1/4 cup nutritional yeast

1/4 cup fresh parsley, minced

1 teaspoon dried thyme

Salt and pepper

1 cup fine whole grain bread crumbs

Two 9-inch pre-packaged pie crusts

## Directions:

Cook the potatoes however you would like, either boiling, microwave, or baking. Set half of the cooked potatoes aside. Mash the other half of the potatoes, set the mashed potatoes aside as well.

Heat the oven to 350 degrees. While the oven is heating, turn the stovetop on medium heat. Warm the oil in a skillet, add the onion and sauté until the onion is cooked.

Add the chopped vegetables into the skillet with the onion. Put a little bit of water in the skillet, cover with the lid, and cook for about 5 minutes. The vegetables should begin to get tender, but they shouldn't be cooked through.

In a small mixing bowl, add the broth, flour and nutritional yeast. Whisk together well, then pour over the vegetables in the skillet. Stir consistently as the sauce starts to turn thicker. Add in the mashed and diced potatoes, as well as the seasonings. Stir well to mix everything together.

Add the potato mixture in the pie crust. Bake for 40 minutes. After removing from the oven, allow the pot pies to sit for 10 minutes before cutting into them.

# Dairy-Free Pizza

## Crust Ingredients:

1 package active dry yeast (.25-ounces)

1 1/2 cups warm water

1 tablespoon sugar

1 teaspoon salt

1 teaspoon extra virgin olive oil

1/2 cup all-purpose flour

2 1/2 cups whole wheat flour

## Topping Ingredients:

3 cloves garlic, minced

1/2 red onion, chopped

1 bell pepper, chopped,

1 - 2 cups mushrooms, sliced

1 cup red pizza sauce

Tomatoes, diced

## Directions:

Add the yeast, sugar, and warm water into a large bowl, stir gently. Cover the bowl with a towel and let it sit for 5 minutes. Next, add in the salt and oil, then slowly add the flour. Add enough flour so that the dough is soft, but not too sticky. Knead the dough for 5 minutes.

Remove the dough from the mixing bowl, spray the mixing bowl with nonstick cooking spray, and then put the dough back in. Cover with a lint-free towel, and let it rise for an hour. The dough should double in size.

After rising, work the dough down with your hands, knead for a few minutes to work it into a ball, then let it rise again for another 45 minutes.

Preheat to 425 degrees. Oil the baking pan with non-stick cooking spray.

Roll the dough out, then arrange it on the baking sheet. add toppings of your choice, bake for 20 minutes.

A good technique for non-dairy pizza toppings is to layer the dough with red sauce, then add the toppings to fill the pizza so there are no remaining empty spaces. If desired, sprinkle a little bit of non-dairy cheese on the top.

# Stuffed Bell Peppers

## Ingredients:

4 bell peppers, seeded and cut in half

1 onion, diced

1 1/2 tablespoons extra virgin olive oil

2 tablespoons chili powder

2 garlic cloves, minced

2 teaspoons paprika

2 teaspoons cumin

3 cups baby spinach, chopped

1 can black beans, rinsed and drained

1 can diced tomatoes

3 cups cooked quinoa

1/4 cup fresh cilantro, chopped

Salt and black pepper

## Directions:

Heat oven to 375 degrees. Prepare the baking dish by spraying generously with nonstick cooking spray.

In a skillet, heat the oil and then add the garlic and onions. Sautee for 5 minutes. Add in the seasonings, cook for another 60 seconds. Then add the tomatoes, quinoa, spinach, and black beans. Stir everything together, cook for 5 minutes.

Remove the skillet from the heat, stir in the cilantro, and spoon the filling into the bell pepper halves.

Place the bell peppers on the greased baking sheet. Bake, covered with foil, for about 25 minutes.

Garnish with fresh cilantro and serve immediately.

# Lentil Casserole

## Ingredients:

2 cups cooked lentils

2 tablespoons extra virgin olive oil

1 onion, diced

1 green pepper, diced

1/2 pound mushrooms, sliced

1 jar spaghetti sauce

1 can tomato sauce

1 teaspoon Italian seasoning

1 pound spaghetti, broken up into pieces

3/4 cup almond milk

2 egg replacer, brand of your choice

1 cup vegan parmesan cheese

## Directions:

Preheat the oven, set the temperature to 350 degrees. Cook the pasta according to the package directions.

In a skillet, heat the oil and then sauté the onion, bell pepper, and mushrooms. Sautee for 5 minutes, then add the tomato sauce, the pasta sauce, and the seasonings. Stir well and simmer for 15 minutes.

In a large mixing bowl, whisk together the egg replacer and almond milk. Add in the pasta and lentils, and toss to evenly coat.

Prepare the casserole dish by spraying with nonstick cooking oil. Add in half of the noodles, then half of the sauce, then the rest of the noodles and top with the remaining sauce.

Cover with tinfoil, and bake the casserole for 1 hour. Sprinkle the vegan parmesan cheese before serving.

# Mini Mexican Pizzas

## Ingredients:

1 cup refried beans

1/3 cup avocado, chopped

1/3 cup bell pepper, chopped

1/3 cup tomatoes, chopped

1/3 cup salsa

spoonful of vegan sour cream

shredded lettuce

whole wheat pitas

## Directions:

On a cookie sheet, lay the pitas flat and spread refried beans on the top of the pitas. Add a few scoops of salsa, spread evenly over the beans. Add the avocado, bell pepper, and tomatoes on top.

Bake at 375 degrees for 10 minutes to warm. Top with lettuce and sour cream before serving.

# Vegan Salad Meals

Even though salads are sometimes thought of as "side dishes," the truth is that they can make a great main meal if they are prepared the right way. Salads are a wonderful option if you are looking for something fresh and healthy on a warm summer day, or they are a fast meal that can be thrown together in a tupperware dish on the way out the door.

Salads offer so many health benefits because they are loaded with vegetables that are high in fiber and nutritional value. They are healthy and tasty, and these recipes have been designed to be filling and satisfying.

# Balsamic Apple Walnut Salad

## Ingredients:

1 romaine heart, chopped

2 cups baby spinach

1/2 cup sprouts

1/2 cup chickpeas

1 apple, cored and chopped

1 tablespoon raisins

1 tablespoon walnuts, chopped

1/2 jalapeno, seeded and minced

2 tablespoons Balsamic Vinaigrette

## Directions:

In a large salad bowl, combine all ingredients. Drizzle the salad dressing over the top, and toss to evenly coat the salad in dressing.

# Black Bean Quinoa Salad

## Ingredients:

1/3 cup quinoa, uncooked

2 tablespoons scallions, minced

4 teaspoons fresh lime juice

1/4 cup cilantro, chopped

1 teaspoon extra virgin olive oil

1/4 teaspoon coriander

1/4 teaspoon cumin

2 cups tomatoes, diced

1 can black beans, drained and rinsed

1 cup orange bell pepper, diced

2 teaspoons jalapeno, seeded and minced

salt and pepper to taste

## Directions:

Cook the quinoa according to package directions. Cool for 20 minutes.

In a large mixing bowl. add the scallions, cilantro, coriander, cumin, lime juice, and olive oil. Whisk together.

Add the bell peppers, jalapeno, tomato, beans and quinoa into the mixing bowl.

Stir well to evenly coat everything with the dressing. Chill in the fridge for at least 2 hours, serve chilled.

# Corn and Black Bean Salad

## Ingredients:

1 can corn, drained

1 can black beans, rinsed and drained

1 tomato, chopped

1/8 cup red onion, chopped

1/4 cup fresh cilantro, chopped

3 tablespoons lemon juice

2 tablespoons olive oil

salt and pepper to taste

Mixed salad greens

## Directions:

Combine everything except the salad greens in a mixing bowl, stir together to mix all ingredients. Chill in the fridge for at least 2 hours. Serve over a bed of leafy greens.

# Artichoke Watercress Salad

## Salad Ingredients:

1 teaspoon extra virgin olive oil

1 red onion, thinly sliced

3 garlic cloves, minced

10 marinated artichoke hearts

1 red bell pepper, sliced

sea salt

2 watercress bunches, stems removed

4 cups grapes, sliced in half

3 scallions, thinly sliced

1/2 cup almonds, slivered or sliced

## Dressing Ingredients:

2 lemons, juiced

1/4 cup extra virgin olive oil

2 teaspoons apple cider vinegar

2 teaspoons Maple Rice Nectar (Suzanne's Specialties)

Pinch black pepper

## Directions:

In a skillet, heat the oil and sauté the onions and garlic for 1 -2 minutes. Add in the artichoke hearts and red bell pepper, sauté for another 2 minutes.

Make the dressing by whisking all of the dressing ingredients together.

Assemble the salad in a large bowl. Put the watercress on the bottom, then add the grapes, followed by the artichoke hearts mixture. Drizzle the dressing over the top, garnish with scallions and almonds. Serve immediately.

# Taco Salad

## Ingredients:

2 tomatoes, diced

1 bell pepper, chopped

1/2 cup black olives, chopped

1 avocado, diced

1 can black beans, rinsed and drained

3 tablespoons sunflower seeds

Mixed greens

Tortilla chips

Garnish with fresh cilantro

Optional: 1 cup grated vegan cheddar cheese

## Dressing Ingredients:

1 lime, juiced

1 tablespoon olive oil

1/3 cup tomato sauce

1/2 teaspoon dried oregano

1/2 teaspoon chili powder

## Directions:

In a small bowl, combine all dressing ingredients and whisk well to combine.

Assemble salads as desired, with the greens on the bottom and topped with all other ingredients. Drizzle dressing over the top, garnish with fresh cilantro.

# Greek Salad

## Ingredients:

2 tablespoons lemon juice

6 tablespoons extra virgin olive oil

1 teaspoon red wine vinegar

1 garlic clove, minced

1 teaspoon fresh dill, chopped

1 teaspoon fresh oregano, chopped

Salt and black pepper, to taste

1 cucumber, peeled and chopped

3 tomatoes, seeded and chopped

1 bell pepper, chopped

1/2 red onion, chopped

1/2 cup kalamata olives, chopped

1/2 cup vegan feta cheese (or any other type of vegan cheese)

Leafy greens of your choice, chopped

## Directions:

In small bowl, stir together the dill weed, oregano, vinegar, garlic, olive oil, lemon juice, pepper and salt.

In a big bowl, add the leafy greens and then top with olives, bell pepper, onion, cucumber, and tomatoes. Pour the dressing over the top and toss to evenly coat the vegetables in dressing. Sprinkle vegan cheese on top and serve immediately.

## Black-Eyed Pea Salad

### Ingredients:

1 cup kalamata olives, chopped

4 cups black eyed peas, cooked

1 garlic clove, chopped

1/2 cup sundried tomatoes, chopped

1/2 cup cilantro, chopped

1 green onion, chopped

Juice and zest of 1 lemon

3 tablespoons extra virgin olive oil

1 large bunch of spinach, chopped

Sea salt, to taste

Optional: vegan feta cheese to garnish

### Directions:

In a large mixing bowl, add the spinach and all other ingredients, finish by drizzling the oil and lemon on top. Toss, and serve immediately.

# Roasted Vegetables and Greens

## Ingredients:

2 yellow squash, chopped

2 zucchini, chopped

1 pound asparagus, chopped

1 red onion, chopped

3 bell peppers, seeded and chopped

2 cups marinated artichoke hearts

1/4 cup red wine vinegar

1/2 cup extra virgin olive oil

2 garlic cloves, minced

1 tablespoon Dijon mustard

salt and black pepper, to taste

Leafy greens of your choice

## Directions:

Chop the vegetables, arrange them evenly on a cookie sheet. Broil the vegetables in the oven for 5 minutes, flip them and continue broiling until they are roasted.

Whisk the dressing in a small bowl. Add the salt and pepper, garlic, mustard, vinegar, and oil together and mix well.

Add the leafy greens in a big mixing bowl, top with the roasted vegetables and drizzle the dressing on top. Toss to coat evenly, serve immediately.

# Tortellini and Broccoli Salad

## Ingredients:

1 package vegan tortellini or ravioli

3 heads broccoli, chopped

6 slices vegan bacon, cooked and crumbled

1/2 cup sugar

1/2 cup vegan mayonnaise

2 teaspoons apple cider vinegar

1 cup sunflower seeds

1 cup raisins

1 red onion, chopped

## Directions:

Cook the tortellini according to the package instructions. In a small bowl, whisk together the vinegar, sugar and mayonnaise.

In a large bowl, combine the broccoli, tortellini, bacon, sunflower seeds, onion and raisins. Pour the dressing on top and toss. Serve immediately.

# Southwestern Rice and Beans

## Ingredients:

2 1/2 cups cooked brown rice, chilled

1 avocado, diced

1 bell pepper, chopped

1 lime, juiced

2 tablespoons red wine vinegar

3 tablespoons extra-virgin olive oil

2 green onions, chopped

1 can black beans, rinsed and drained

1/4 cup fresh cilantro, chopped

1/2 teaspoon dried oregano

1 teaspoon chili powder

## Directions:

Add all ingredients into a large mixing bowl, stir well to mix everything together. Garnish with lime wedges.

# Artichoke Asparagus Salad

## Ingredients:

2 pounds roasted asparagus, chopped

1 jar marinated artichoke hearts, roughly chopped

1/4 cup red onion, thinly sliced

3 tablespoons lemon juice

2 tablespoons extra virgin olive oil, divided

1 pint grape or cherry tomatoes, cut in half

1 teaspoon garlic powder

1/2 cup walnuts, chopped

Salt and pepper to taste

Leafy greens of your choice

## Directions:

Soak the onions in lemon juice while you are preparing the rest of the salad.

Roast the asparagus: by tossing it in the olive oil, then bake at 400 degrees on a cookie sheet. Cook for about 10 minutes.

In a large bowl, add the leafy greens first, then top with the rest of the ingredients. Add a few spoonfuls of the juice from the artichoke jar, to taste. Serve immediately.

# Orzo Tomato Salad

## Ingredients:

8 ounces uncooked orzo pasta

2 pints cherry tomatoes (1 red and 1 yellow), sliced in half

1/4 cup extra virgin olive oil

2 green onions, sliced

1 cucumber, chopped

1 lemon, juiced

2 tablespoons fresh oregano, minced

salt and black pepper to taste

8 ounces nondairy cheese, crumbled

Leafy greens of your choice

## Directions:

Cook the orzo according to package directions. Drain the hot water, rinse with cold water, and drain well.

Add the orzo into a large mixing bowl, combine with all other ingredients except the leafy greens. Toss to combine

Chill in the fridge for at least 2 hours. Serve on a bed of leafy greens.

# Chinese Salad

## Ingredients:

1 head of green leaf lettuce or Napa cabbage, chopped

4 green onions, sliced

1 red bell pepper, chopped

1 cup garbanzo beans

1 carrot, chopped

1 small cans mandarin oranges, drained

1/2 cup cilantro leaves, chopped

1/4 cup peanuts, roasted

1/4 cup almonds, slivered

Garnish with crunchy chow mein noodles

## Dressing Ingredients:

1/4 cup peanut oil

2 tablespoons rice vinegar

1 teaspoon fresh ginger, grated

1 teaspoon mustard powder

1/2 teaspoon chili pepper flakes

1 garlic clove, minced

1 tablespoon dark sesame oil

2 teaspoons brown sugar

## Directions:

Make the dressing by whisking all dressing ingredients in a small bowl.

Prepare the salad in a large mixing bowl. Add the greens, top with other ingredients, drizzle dressing over the top. Toss to evenly coat the salad in the dressing.

# Vegan Cobb Salad

## Ingredients:

1/2 head of romaine, chopped

1 small bunch curly endive, chopped

1/2 head of leafy red lettuce, chopped

1/2 bunch of watercress, stems removed, chopped

1 cup non-dairy cheese, shredded

6 slices of vegan bacon, cooked and crumbled

1 tomato, chopped

2 ripe avocados, diced

2 tablespoons green onions, chopped

## Dressing Ingredients:

2/3 cup extra virgin olive oil

1/3 cup red wine vinegar

1 tablespoon Dijon mustard

2 teaspoons sugar

Salt and pepper

## Directions:

Wash, dry and chop the greens. Toss them together in a large bowl.

Arrange the toppings by decoratively adding all of the ingredients.

Whisk the dressing ingredients together, then drizzle over the top of the salad. Serve immediately.

# Chilled Curry Rice

## Ingredients:

2 cups cold rice, cooked

1 cup celery, chopped

1 cup carrots, chopped

1/2 cup onion, chopped

1/2 cup corn

1/2 cup peas

1/3 cup slivered almonds

Leafy green vegetables of your choice

## Dressing Ingredients:

1 tablespoon soy sauce

1/4 cup extra virgin olive oil

1 teaspoon sugar

1 teaspoon curry powder

1 teaspoon apple cider vinegar

## Directions:

In a small bowl, add the dressing ingredients and whisk well. In a large mixing bowl, add all ingredients except the almonds leafy greens. Drizzle the dressing on top of the rice mixture, and toss to evenly coat.

Serve on a bed of leafy greens, with the almonds on top for garnish.

Made in the USA
San Bernardino, CA
04 May 2014